MAKING, MANAGING & MULTIPLYING MONEY

LEARN HOW TO MAXIMISE YOUR MONEY-MAKING POTENTIALS

Volume 1

VINCENT A NWALI (MBA, B.SC.)

Copyright © 2018 Vincent A Nwali (MBA, B.SC.) All rights reserved. No part of this book may be reproduced, stored in a retrieval system, or transmitted in any form or by any means, electronic, mechanical, photocopying, recording, scanning, or otherwise, without the prior written permission of the publisher.

DEDICATION

I dedicate this book to many mentors I have listened to for many years.

CONTENTS

DEDICATION III

WHY I WROTE THIS BOOK XV

1: HOW TO ACHIEVE YOUR LIFE GOALS.............. 1

2: QUESTION TO ASK YOURSELF BEFORE SETTING YOUR LIFE GOALS 13

3: FURTHER QUESTIONS TO ASK YOURSELF .. 25

4: CHANGE WHEN EVERYTHING ELSE FAILS ... 39

5: YOU MUST HAVE THE MIND-SET OF AN ENTREPRENEUR 47

6: ACHIEVING YOUR FINANCIAL DREAM 63

7: THE LAWS OF MONEY 77

WHY I WROTE THIS BOOK

Poverty is a condition of the mind, a product of your belief system. You can't be doing the same thing over and over again and expect changes in your life. They call it insanity. If what you believe is not producing for you then you need to change your belief system; It's as simple as that.

The poor has 24hrs a day, so also is the rich. Hence the difference between the poor and rich is what they put into their time. What you are continuously listening to you are believing, and what you are believing you are rapidly becoming.

There is so much opportunity for everyone in this our age, but there is also information overload. That's why I wrote this book to distil for you the finest money-making principle that anyone can apply immediately and begin to see instant results in your finances.

These principles are a product of many years of sitting under the feet of many accomplished mentors, listening, taking notes and doing. They work.

I believe in giving back, because in doing so we increase more. This book is a seed into your life, and if you would studiously read the seven chapters again and again your life will never be the same. Just one principle in this book will turn your life around forever.

Note that I didn't mention college qualifications here, and you may not see it inside the book as prerequisite for you to start making money, because it's not. Your passion and willingness to learn is by far more important. You are your only advantage or disadvantage.

Vincent
CEO
Money Matters (http://financiercenter.com)

1

HOW TO ACHIEVE YOUR LIFE GOALS

Achieving your life goals is the meaning success, but attaining successes is a function of attitude rather than circumstances. All our actions are preceded by a desire to gain an advantage or to avoid one. Habits manifest when we do things that we didn't really want to do. The clearer your motive, the stronger your desire. Build motives based on lasting principles. Integrity is the key to developing stronger will power. There is a price (time, effort and sacrifice of yourself) to pay in order to succeed – inexorably, but it must establish a return greater than the original cost. Never contemplate immediate, cheap merchandise (product or service) that is ill-fitting and short-lived. Apply same to goal setting. It's not the more advanced information I can collect that determines how successful I can become; it's the relevance and application of what I know that leads to success.

Positioning

Positioning – points to timing, location, markets, the economy, shortages and world events. You can position yourself by studying trends, markets and ability to decipher hidden opportunities.

Rules of Good Positioning

1. Be an initiator – somewhere, somehow unique opportunity exists where you could provide a service or solve a problem.

3 LEARN HOW TO MAXIMISE YOUR MONEY-MAKING POTENTIALS

2. Recognise, change and shift yourself accordingly to act as a pivot point. Make it a life time pattern.
3. Maintain control in every situation – Refuse to be buffeted by circumstances. Stand your ground.
4. Refuse Greed – ask yourself this question: 'If I sold now, would there be something left for someone else?'
5. Gravitate always towards areas where you want to operate – politics, business, ministry, etc.
6. Avoid suspicion and over caution.
7. If you kept failing over and over one thing it's because you've not properly mastered it.
8. Don't break well learned proven principles.
9. You have to be willing to accept exposure to dangers, failures, embarrassments and ridicules sometimes to achieve security, success, confidence and esteem.

Your Person Personality Matters

- Develop a people person personality – he remembers names, recalls events and previous meetings.
- Become gregarious, develop conversational skills and get on with people.
- Become a book person – be fascinated and attracted by books that develop and inspire.
- Reading expands one's life.
- Everyone has a style – what you do and the way you do it. Add flair to your style that causes you to stand out e.g. when making a presentation.
- A healthy body reflects a healthy mind: in other words, healthy body can do what the mind requires.
- Exercise daily and pay attention to what we eat.
- Concentration/focus requires dedication, desperation and no interruption – concentration disturbs peace and freedom.

5 LEARN HOW TO MAXIMISE YOUR MONEY-MAKING POTENTIALS

Refuse the Comfort Trap

- Refuse to languish in comfort.
- Your deportment matters – the way you carry yourself; etiquette.
- Clothes don't make the man, but they certainly introduce him.
- When working on developing new habits whether it relates to your mind, attitude and/or appearance never let an exception occur.
- The crowd is always wrong. Find out the direction they are going and take the opposite direction. A man in singular is unusual and unpredictable but a man in the crowd is easy to predict and evaluate.
- Crowds can absorb energy and waste time.
- Goals are the solidification of dreams, ideas and ideals in practical form, for practical implementation for practical completion. It's the result of bringing dreams, ideas and ideals into tangible and examinable form.
- Solidify your dreams with the written word.

- Goals require maps. The map must be as explicit and clear as possible with as much detail packed in as possible.

Dreaming

Dreaming is simply birthing something out of nothing. Setting life goals requires that you imagine your life and the world up to ten, twenty, forty, fifty years into the future. In so doing you excite your senses and reawaken your spirit to the greatness within you.

Do not be too busy to dream, rather be busy dreaming. Cut your heavy schedules and go alone to a quiet spot with a pen and paper or tape recorder and dream, imagine, plot. Talk to yourself and think.

The distance we can travel intellectually is directly related to the size of our dreams and the belief we have in them.

7 LEARN HOW TO MAXIMISE YOUR MONEY-MAKING POTENTIALS

Dream & Purpose

Big dreams give purpose and big purpose promotes self-esteem and dignity.

Purpose in dreaming puts the emphasis on the reason for achieving, and that is a point that should be remembered. While dreaming and planning, the honesty factor must be totally clean, and the value system reaffirmed at all levels. A purpose forced into a dream, however worthy, is unworthy for any dream and it will eventually force itself out it.

Clear out of your mind of selfishness, greed, gain for gains' sake and any thought of manipulating others or the system. Let your dream be full of purpose, pure of intent and big in dimensions which will honour God and yourself and inspire all who participate.

In every endeavour watch out for cheap advice or experience that in the long run becomes expensive. The life that you put into your dream by affirmation and enthusiasm will eventually capture you in its net. No dream in reality goes as easily as the visionary dream. Getting launched is the hardest part. Don't confuse false starts and delays with failure. Never seek to make excuses – look to find and fix the problem.

Dreams get shattered by distractions or diversion of interest under all kinds of good and even benevolent disguises. Early disappointment can be very helpful by alerting you to unrecognised problem, preventing a major catastrophe further down the line.

You Must Be Determined

Disappointments are the testing times. They provide opportunities to evaluate your resolves and test your determination quotient before the next step. You only become a permanent failure when you have decided to give up.

Keep your focus on your life goal.

9 LEARN HOW TO MAXIMISE YOUR MONEY-MAKING POTENTIALS

Your Quality Is in Your Uniqueness

Your best cannot be done by someone else. It's unique to you and only cashable by you; not to spend it means the world is the poorer.

Life is worth our best effort, and we need to be committed to plan for it.

The absence of goals is probably one of the most destructive forces facing some people. A life of drifting comes from lack of goals and deadlines. Absence of pressure to meet a timetable through a fulfilled commitment creates sloppiness.

Your energy thrust, or lack of it, is in direct proportion to your most desired or feared task.

Telling your spouse about certain life you are going through will only double the trouble because she would start worrying about you.

Invest in Others

The key to successful life goal is to allow time to support others. There is no substitute to sharing yourself with others.

Handling Criticism

- Remember the biggest critic generally does the least work.
- Paying attention to your critics validates their claim and elevates them.
- Ignoring your critics saves time and energy.
- Never criticise a critic.

Preparing for Your Life Goals

In preparing your simple life goals' formula, build in reserves;

- spiritual,
- physical,
- people,
- emotional/mental and

11 LEARN HOW TO MAXIMISE YOUR MONEY-MAKING POTENTIALS

- financial reserves.

Finally

Eliminate '**asap** ', '**earliest convenience** ', '**urgently** ', etc, from your vocabulary. Be time specific in your correspondences.

As you move through life, set aside good ideas and give them to others to encourage and inspire.

VINCENT A NWALI (MBA, B.SC.) **12**

2

QUESTION TO ASK YOURSELF BEFORE SETTING YOUR LIFE GOALS

Questions create answers and are the cure for confusion. Until you ask questions your knowledge is accidental. You will never know what others know until you ask question. Deceivers will continue to hide from you until you ask questions.

Your key to success is in asking right questions.

A single question can instantly increase the value of a moment in your life. Unasked questions, poor attitude, refusal to follow instructions will keep you poor.

Ask questions until you;

- know what you want right now,
- what you don't want,
- discover what you want to change,
- what you can't live without,
- identify what you hate, fear, enjoy
- who you resent and why you resent them.

Asking questions is the most important thing you can do daily. Until you ask questions you will not know what you truly want in your life.

Every long outstanding issue continues because you are not asking questions enough. Every significant question you ask will create a significant change.

Increasing your questions increases your solutions. Past questions created your present, new questions will create your future.

15 LEARN HOW TO MAXIMISE YOUR MONEY-MAKING POTENTIALS

Master the art of asking the unexpected questions relentlessly. Increase is a factor of questions.

Questions Leads to Effective Decision Making

Questions make decisions easy. It increases your value to others and are the magnet for information. Information is the secret of making effective decisions. Effective decisions eliminate my stress and improves my output. success depends on my decisions. Decisions increases/decides my joy or stress. Your decision making is making you a millionaire or a pauper. The better your questions the better your decisions.

Question will take you to where you have never dreamt of going. To master the secret of life is to make master one more question.

You don't have to have a PhD to be a millionaire, you only need to ask the right questions. Pride is the reason people don't ask questions. You actually have a secret fear of someone knowing what you don't know.

Who is diminishing your energy and making you poor?

- Anyone who crushes you emotionally is deciding your financial future, and it's not in a positive way. Stay away from those whose presence you feel unworthy, and whose words tear you apart.

What part of you is bringing displeasure to God?

- Are you living with a guilty mind as a result of your indulgence in a secret sin? It's something you have to deal with, and that very urgently, because unstable mind is an unproductive life.
- Are you bothered about after life? Why not find out the truth about the true God. It will save you a lifetime of confusion and error.

17 LEARN HOW TO MAXIMISE YOUR MONEY-MAKING POTENTIALS

What small changes on your part will remove your present stress, make a big difference in your life, bring a huge change in your life, and when will you make those changes?

Small keys turn the bank vaults. little changes here and there in your life can bring about big changes. It could be to;

- stop lying,
- start eating right and exercising
- stop making same mistake twice
- start reading again

What are you willing to live without and what price are you willing to pay for it?

- There is a price you are paying for every decision you are making. It's a choice to stay poor but consider the people around you that are being affected by that your singular decision. Some of them cannot go to college because they lack sponsorship; some can't pay their house rents because they are jobless. Those are high costs, and the crushing pain of it alone is enough to desire and seek a change. Let your choices go beyond yourself.

If you were your worst enemy, how would you destroy you?

- By asking this question, you'll understand how to fortify your defence against your enemy, competitors and/or rivals.

What is your greatest passion, and what do you invest daily in its pursuit?

- Your passion is a clue to where your money is. You have to understood it and how to nurture it.

Whose presence energises you?

- You need cheerleaders in your life race. Encouragers will help you strengthen your chosen passion. Keep around you those whose presence propel you towards right causes. There are people that energise you towards sin. Mark them and disconnect from them.

Who has recognised your divine assignment and honoured it significantly?

- Reward those that have helped you succeed.

What would you choose to do with your life if money were not an issue?

- Money is important but don't let it run your life, because money is a cruel master. Master is meant to serve you and not you serving it. Take away money from the equation of your life what remains is who you truly are.

If you could master any topic, what would it be?

- What do you like reading about, talking about, etc.

What problem do you solve best?

- ...even when you are not paid to solve it.

What should you be doing to protect your mind?

- Your mind is the most important thing about you. Who and what you are today are as a result of what entered your mind yesterday, and who and what you become tomorrow will be because of what you are putting in your mind today. Hence you have to consciously guard against what's gaining entry into your mind.

21 LEARN HOW TO MAXIMISE YOUR MONEY-MAKING POTENTIALS

What can't you live without and what price are you willing to pay for it?

- Is your present earning enough, if not what price will you pay to improve it? Time? Effort? More Information? Disciple? New skills? New contacts?

What must you change to obtain the change you long for?

- Do you need to relocate? Do you need to learn computers. Do you need to work part time to reallocate time to learn new skills? You may need to change your job to align with your desired skill? What do you need to prioritise?

What are you refusing to pursue with passion?

- Are you neglecting your passion because you need to survive? Focusing on your passion may be all you need to achieve financial freedom.

What are you refusing to make my life quest?

- You exist for a reason; it's called purpose. If you are not pursuing your purpose, nobody is doing it, which means someone is missing out on your gifts, which also means the world is worse off for it.

What is pride costing you?

- Pride means among other things '...feelings of superiority...', which hinders one from learning from other people. Maybe you think you are too old, or too educated, or whatever reason..., if you cannot learn from another person it's a big problem.

What is your deepest fear and what is it costing you?

- We rationalise our fears to justify them, but it's important to dig deep to find your deepest fears through asking yourself questions of these nature.

What could you be wrong about?

- You may have been misinformed about something and you probably have lived with it all your life. Longevity will never right falsehood. You need to go through your belief system especially if they have not been producing for you to change them.

VINCENT A NWALI (MBA, B.SC.) **24**

3

FURTHER QUESTIONS TO ASK YOURSELF

Question reveal passion, pursuit and humility. It also reveals your desires and needs. You can only enter into any meaningful dialogue or negotiations by asking questions.

In continuation from chapter 2, I have added more questions to ask yourself in your journey towards being a millionaire.

What do I know with no occurring doubt?

- What are your convictions or principles that are unchangeable?

Who do I need to forgive and what is un-forgiveness costing me?

- Un-forgiveness is unnecessary weight to carry. You need to forgive people that wronged you or that you wronged for your own good. It will free your mind to be more creative and consequently more productive.

What changes have I been delaying and when will I make them?

- Procrastination is the destroyer of destinies. Refuse to sit on the changes you need to make to turn your life around. Take steps towards them and see what happens.

27 LEARN HOW TO MAXIMISE YOUR MONEY-MAKING POTENTIALS

What is your future that you are presently investing in?

- What future are you envisaging for your life and what are you doing about it? Will it require a certain kind of training, mentorship of formal education? Does it require you to meet someone you never met before? Will it need a college degree? But are you doing anything in that regards?

What hidden prejudice is harming you?

- Prejudices first and foremost holds you bound; which means you are not seeing things clearly as you should. You must be open minded and free to other people's opinion irrespective of their religion, race, culture, colour, background, or educational attainment. Prejudice is a limiting factor in your life.

What missing conversation could really change everything for me now?

- Who do you need to talk to about your present circumstances? Do you have access to their materials; audio tapes, videos, books, etc.?

What counsel do you pursue; do you pursue it legally, ethically and consistently?

- It matters whose counsel you pursue, because it will decide your future.

Who pursues you advise?

- They are your protégé; the ones you are called to. Pay attention to them.

Who pursues my comfort?

- Mark them and greatly reward them.

Who is dedicated to removing the discomfort in my life?

- That's the person you want around you at all cost.

What serious changes have you made in the last 90 days?

- Refuse to routinize complacency. Continuously evaluate yourself.

Whose favour matters to you; what's the price of keeping at it, and what's the price of losing it?

- Love is expensive to maintain. There's nothing like something for nothing. Everything has a price tag. You either pay the price or lose it.

Whose advice do you follow?

- Anyone you are listening to you are believing, and what you are believing you are becoming.

Whose loyalty have you not rewarded?

- Reward those that helped you to your next level in life.

Does accuracy and integrity matter to you?

- They are the most important capital you need.

What do I want to become next?

- It will require goal setting.

Where should I invest in most?

- Your mind, for then will you be able to help other people.

31 LEARN HOW TO MAXIMISE YOUR MONEY-MAKING POTENTIALS

Who should I invest in now?

- In yourself; your mind.

Where should you invest next?

- Your single most important investment is your mind

Where do you see your increase; where do you try becoming more; wisdom, money, love, favour, peace, productivity?

- Identify where you are lacking and seek it.

Who do I consult when making major decisions?

- Do you make decisions alone? You need inner circle of people whom you can trust to seek their opinions – qualified persons.

What are you willing to change; stop doing?

- What you are willing to stop doing is as important as what you are willing to start doing.

Who are you willing to pursue; who has what you need; information, job, money, etc?

- It's called mentorship. You might need someone to stand on their shoulder who has gone where you want to go, done what you want to do, have what you want to have.

Who are you willing to train for the future comfort of my own life?

- Your future is in who you are willing to train.

What would I attempt to do if I knew it was impossible to fail?

- Starting by paying attention to what you are willing to do without getting paid for it.

Is it really necessary to work like a slave to live like a millionaire?

- Not quite. You can actually work like a king and live like a millionaire. It's your choice.

How do your decisions change if retirement isn't an option?

- Are just living and working for your retirement? If retirement was not a factor, what could you have done differently? That's the real you.

What is your life purpose – Mission Statement?

- A mission statement can be described as a written statement of purpose, behaviour and boundaries where there is the life pursuit. A mission statement is the style of pursuit. It sets a pattern of behaviour that exhibits a character of an organisation or a person. Also, mission statement creates relationships and culture of an organisation or a person; it is the anchor in the stormy seas of life.

What do you need to get the job done through education, position, influence, and finance?

- Determining what's required to get from point A to point B?

What is your exit point?

- You must not continue in something that's not working wasting time and other resources. There should be a time to make a change or go in another direction.

What specific commitments are you prepared to make in time, talent and treasure?

- Anything worthwhile will cost you something – time, talent and money. Are you prepared to incur them?

What time will it terminate without your continued input – running of your business?

- You must aim at your business operating without your day to day input to enable you engage in other projects.

Are you measuring your progress repeatedly?

- You must continuously evaluate the results of your present effort.

Is my work habit consistent?

- Anything you do twice becomes easier. We are creatures of habit. You develop new or destroy bad habits. Consciously work on anything until it becomes habitual.

What's the one thing I can do right now to create a consistent work habit, so that by doing it, everything else becomes easier or unnecessary?

- Find a focus and pour all of you into it.

Are your mistakes repetitive?

- You certainly have not understood it if a common mistake continues to occur.

What necessities do you have to routinized?

- Outsource necessary repetitive tasks to free your time for more productive use.

4

CHANGE WHEN EVERYTHING ELSE FAILS

The Virus Called Fear That Stops Change

Change occurs when you become more daring. Fear is the virus ravaging the non-achievers. The one that thinks he is a failure is terrified of change. Startled by the challenge of change. Change will always be part of human events. We must accept change to progress in life.

You must aim to take your rightful place in the world affairs as a guide to the nations, as a seasoning to the people, as a leader in economics and as a light to morality.

What if you tried and tried and tried again and everything you touched just goes wrong and you've fallen severally on your face. Nothing seems to work.

What to Do To Cause Change When Nothing Seems To Work

- The first thing to do when all your dreams are fallen into a heap is to discover your second wind. We need resilience to rise again to our feet.
- Secondly, you have to repair your broken principles. When everything collapses all around you, you have broken a principle(s).

Creating A Change Requires Four Laws

1. **Truth is usually the first casualty in every conflict.** It conquers everything, and its inconvertible. Panic may resent it, ignorance may deride it, malice may distort it but there it is. The failure to observe truth is the cause of all broken relationship. Truth is the foundation of all sound judgment. Truth is the basis of all moral laws.
2. **The second law is the law of love**. Love never fails. If it's not working double the dose. The first step in love is to accept yourself. The next step in love is to accept others. Create a passion to be a catalyst for hope to the hurting and misguided world.
3. **The third law is power**. The power to absorb. What is your power of absorption intelligent quotient. The power to dream. Without the spirit there is no dream and there is nothing as pathetic as dispossessed spirit. The other thing

is power to perform. Productivity is inseparably tied to purity. How long do you wish to exist in the basement of your life? You must have the urgency factor. Finally, is the discipline to do your best and to beat it.
4. **The fourth part is commitment** – Every act has it's spiritual, economic and social implication. The spirit is not separate, and it can never be.

How to Achieve Your Goals

1. **Develop a decisive plan:** if you set a long-term goal and put your heart and your mind in it, it will actually re-programme your body clock. Don't fiddle around with 4, 10, 15, 20-year goals because you lose the motivation. The mission is the ethics and mechanics of the journey. The goal is the end result.
2. **Create a mission statement**: a mission statement can be described as a written statement of purpose, behaviour and boundaries where there is the life pursuit. A

mission statement is the style of pursuit; it sets a pattern of behaviour that exhibits a character of an organisation or a person. A mission statement creates relationships and culture of an organisation or a person. It is the anchor in the stormy seas of life.

3. **Knowing what you want to achieve:** what you want to transfer your life for is the 75% of its fulfilment, but most people are raring to go but cannot go for the raring.
- What do you need to get the job done through education, position, influence and finance?
- Do you see exit points?
- How big do you want it in measurable terms? Time partition is of crucial importance.
- What specific commitments are you prepared to make in time, talent and treasure?
- Will it satisfy your inner yearnings?
- A what time will it terminate without your continued input?

- Do you live your life by adopting priority economics?
- Are you alert to exit options?
- Dreams without plans are mere fancy. Can you see the full picture?
- You have to renew, refresh reinvigorate and rediscover your discipline quotient.

Causing Change Through Will Power

A weak will power destroys your;

- honesty factor,
- self-esteem and
- relationships.

You must have a bigger reason to do and not to do. Will power is freedom within boundaries.

Guard Yourself for the Long Haul When Going Through Change.

People look at you and see where you are presently, but can't see how far you can go, the same with IQ test. The questions to ask yourself are;

- have you been measuring your progress repeatedly?
- are your mistakes repetitive?
- Is your work habit inconsistent?
- have you routine your necessities?

Create check points that are realistic – you may have to expand your mind. Man have an incredible capacity to adjust downward. When things happen adversely, we tend to withdraw and tighten our belts, but you have to square up and push on. You must never accept defeat. Push the boundaries out. Your darkest hour may precede your greatest hopes. You should always come with a sense of the future and you should have a realistic understanding of your position and your capacity. How much of yourself are you prepared to give? What is the size of your dreams?

- Defeat is just a stepping stone to victory.
- Failure is a progression towards success.
- poverty is a springboard to riches.

Efforts, goals, disciplines, dreams, faith and character are the essence of champions.

5

YOU MUST HAVE THE MIND-SET OF AN ENTREPRENEUR

An Entrepreneur according Dictionary.com is defined as a person who organizes and manages any enterprise, especially a business, usually with considerable initiative and risk.

Important terms to understand

Ethos - the moral character, the source of his or her ability to persuade.

Pathos - the ability to touch feelings and move people emotionally.

Logos - the ability to give solid reason for an action and move people intellectually.

A leader does not get distracted by issues away from main events, he uses time and energy out of proportion to the dominant cause.

- An Entrepreneur is prepared to accept immediate deprivation in exchange for future gratification.
- The Entrepreneur have deep sense of reality to the urgent.
- Entrepreneurs are prepared to accept failures with insight and optimism.
- An Entrepreneur attains and use that attainment and share it with others.
- The Entrepreneur very often move from crisis to crisis, losing some, winning others, and gaining ground at every opportunity.

Persistence

- You should never give up or let up or shut up until you achieve your desired goal. Be ready to approach 5000 banks until you get that loan.
- The problem successful people had to overcome, the difficulty they had to wrestle with gave them the seasoning and information and the ability to do what they are doing today.
- Worry is creating mental pictures of the things that you do not want.

Decision Making

- Do not permit dissenters to be your decision makers.
- Successful people make decisions quickly and change them rarely, while unsuccessful people make decisions slowly and change them very often.

Reserves

- If you need to go into business, you need to have financial reserves. They should be for catastrophes not for new cars.

Sales Commission

- Sales people around the world are often the most unsuccessful, because they cannot handle rejection. If you can handle rejection you will succeed. Go into sales and do it on commission only and see yourself rise to the top.

The Power of Choice

- The greatest gift God has given us is the power of choice.

Law and Conflict: How to Navigate Them as An Entrepreneur

- It's important you don't sue and not be sued by anyone. There are many conflicts but it's better

to settle out of court than to go before the unjust judges.
- Law does not necessarily provide justice; it creates forum for contest and the best story teller with supported believable evidence wins the lottery.
- There is a natural conflict of interest with every lawyer because there is obvious economic benefit for them to prolong the struggle.
- Law only provides a contest. All legal procedures are done by case laws.
- If you are in litigation ask your lawyer for a percentage opinion on a successful conclusion based on similar cases experienced by him or her in case law.
- Always get cost analysis in writing on steps to be taken with limit on variables.
- When they tell you no-fee, no-win, bear in mind what they don't tell you that if you lose you'd have to pay the legal cost of your opponent.

- In a major conflict, get 3 professional opinions, 3 estimates and pay each of them individually against the other two.
- In law and conflict the best advice is Matthew 5:25, agree early (settle out of court) even if it cost you something.

Getting Loan from Banks

- If you need a £100,000, borrow £200,000. Put the extra £100,000 in a non-aligned bank somewhere else. That's your reserve. So, when everything goes wrong, the bank will not be able to squeeze you into a corner as you will be able to debate with them from a position of strength and not weakness. Banks to a large extent don't have money, they lend credit.
- Only one out of 250 people are debt free conservatively in the western worlds.
- You can always argue with banks. They are willing to negotiate.

Borrowing Money from Banks As An Entrepreneur

When you want to borrow money from banks you need 12 major statements;

- the size of the market that you are going for.
- the size of your target market.
- the method of marketing.
- the quality of your competition.
- the gross, net and variables of costs
- the estimated timing of events – when is the business going to open, when are you going to supply staff, when are you going to buy and deploy equipment, when are you going to market, when are you going to pay everything back.
- the in-house management system – the internal and financial control system you intend to adopt, the CRM, the organisational structure.
- the profit anticipated – always put down a lower figure than you are expecting.

- your relative proven, past experience – important
- your exist options – lease agreements.
- tell them what the limiting factors are.
- the cash required.

The 12 Principles of Entrepreneurship

- Drive - they will keep going when everyone has given up and gone home.
- They are persuasive - they have the quest to get others to see how they can follow through with their point of view.
- Perception - Entrepreneurs see what are not distinguishable to others; they believe what others find unbelievable.
- They have strong egos which compel them to win sometimes at any cost.
- Entrepreneurs respond to failures and crisis with optimism.
- Confidence - they have confidence in their own ability to adjust and win from changing circumstances.

- Entrepreneurs know what their inner beliefs can permit them to do.
- They plan strategies and measure their progress continually.
- Entrepreneurs have short term view when assessing performance and long-term view when assessing success.
- Their final destination is clear, measurable, specific, timed, quality and quantitative values.
- They are mentally accurate and objectively urgent in all their deliberations.
- Entrepreneurs tend to choose people to assist them with the strength they do not have to fill in their gap.

Financial Formulae for Economic Protection

- Get out of debt as soon as practicable and stay up.
- Avoid situations where your financial future depends absolutely on borrowed money.

- Refuse to get involved in land, lease or other commitments where debt will rise and expand with interest rate or maintenance cost.
- Never enter into any agreement without you having total control.
- Build reserves of cash and precious metals exclusive of all other commitments.
- Never allow your reserve to become collaterals.
- Do not allow anyone to have control over your finances.
- Keep a minimum of 20% of your asset in cash and precious metals.
- Never permit easy access to your assets…

Principles of Running A Business

- the first thing you have to understand about running a business is you must not make a loss; you are absolutely responsible for everything, and;
- make sure you pay yourself regularly.
- work on basis of minimal debt.
- keep sensible deadlines.

57 LEARN HOW TO MAXIMISE YOUR MONEY-MAKING POTENTIALS

- Pick responsible & capable staff.
- Don't pick your cousin. Don't give your brother in-law a job because he's broke. If you love him that much, give him £200/month to stay home. Let him not mess up your business.
- Never surrender your authority.
- Pay your staff well.
- Only expect and tolerate excellence and make no rash promises when the business is going well that you may find hard to keep when you have downturn in business.
- Attack problems quickly. Apologise and send expensive gifts.
- Don't believe everything you are told, when your own staff tells you anything qualify it.
- Make your staff bear the cost of their errors.
- Do not have everything your business own under the same legal entity; split everything up, because if someone sues you they can only get one of them. Don't make it so that all the docks

fold up one time, make sure you've got all broken up.
- Be careful, don't let anyone litigate their way into your business.
- Be careful of honouring fools. You can lose more to fools than you lose to crooks.
- Beware of Christians; not all Christians tell the truth, not all of them have good work ethics, some of them are just lazy bums.

Franchising

An entrepreneur must understand that franchising is a good way to go into business, but you have to ask the 12 questions that are essential to franchising business;

- Ascertain if it's well established, 10 years or over?
- Is it recently established.
- Verify if it's in decline and ran its course?
- Are there any entry or training fees?
- Is head office providing ongoing support?

- Are there any loans or advances available?
- The percentage of net or gross profit to the head office?
- Is there any budget input from head office for franchise advertising?
- Is there franchise advisory board?
- How is assessment carried out on selection of location and territory?
- Is there support system profiled for difficult franchise? and
- Are all promises made in writing with penalties both ways?

How Do You Buy A Business?

- Beware of the goodwill mystic – there is a lot of caveat emptor (let the buyer beware).
- If the business has been operating for about 20 years successfully, don't change the name just to get an ego rob.
- Try hard to understand the kind of business that you are into. The ideal business is the kind you

can start and stop whenever you wanted. It's the type that generates high income with minimal effort, and this is achievable mainly on selling businesses.
- Is the product 40% better than anything else in the entire world? That way you have absolutely no one competing against you. You can charge what you like and do whatever you want.
- Eliminate competition.

How to Read Books

- What is your mission in life; what are you going to trade your life for? Dream or no dream you are trading your life for something whether or not you know it.
- Don't become wasteful information gatherer.
- If God has not called, you to be a mechanic while fiddle around with mechanics?
- If you can establish what your mission is in life you can read faster than anything you considered possible in life.

61 LEARN HOW TO MAXIMISE YOUR MONEY-MAKING POTENTIALS

- As you read you only have to look for 3 things if you know what your mission in life is.
- Information relative to your mission in life – be careful what you put in your brain.
- Look for principles – they are things that endure – family commitments, responsibilities in the house of God, duties to others are some of the things that should never change.
- Key phrases. Words are tools of trade. Study words. Words can change anyone's life.
- Flip through all the books you have read sometimes in case you have forgotten something.

6

ACHIEVING YOUR FINANCIAL DREAM

Dream is anything you wants you to

- become,
- do, and/or
- have,

during your lifetime.

Your dream will not make everybody happy. Sometimes it agitates people. When Joseph (in the Bible) saw himself in authority and his brothers bowing down to him, he told his brothers about it. Because any dream you can contain is not big enough to move you. When you have an obsession, it will enter every conversation, and reflect in everything you do. It'll overcome you and overwhelm you. You'll talk about it even if it activates adversary. If you have a strong desire inside you, it'll drive you from where you are to where you want to be. Your desire determines what you are willing to overcome, leave, or walk away from. Let your obsession control you, overwhelm you.

Your Financial Dream Will Require Faith

No one can help you until you decide what you want to do with your life. Do you have a picture, because faith has to have a picture? You can complain, bellyache, and get upset, but it won't change anything. Have a picture. Change in your life will not occur until you change the picture inside you. You want a nice house! Where do you want to live? You want more money! How much more?

Faith requires an instruction.

Your Financial Dream Is Your Difference

Your financial obsession is the one that separates you from others. You must major on your difference. Your financial desire is what makes you unlike the person nearest to you. Your difference is not in your nationality. It is not in your IQ. It's neither in your gender nor in your race. If your difference is in your being female, then there are more than three billion more like you on the earth. Your point of difference with another person is the dream that is dominant in your mind. The dream determines what you see and endure. It births your tenacity and persistence. Your financial obsession must be believed and pursued before it can come to pass.

Destiny is possible, but it's not inevitable.

The Proof of Desire Is Pursuit

Anything not in your life is something you have not pursued. You only have around you what you consider valuable. Whatever is missing in your life is what you have not truly valued. The proof of desire is pursuit. Your desire is like a seed in your heart now. That obsession can begin with whatever is in your heart today. It may look as though you will never achieve that dream, as if you will never get there, but it starts with just a seed of thought. Stop inventorying what you do not have. Inventory what you have, because what you have will create what you desire. There will never be a day in your life that you have nothing, but you must inventory what you have, because something in your present will create something in your future. Therefore, stop looking at something you do not have and be looking at something you have. It's Your Responsibility.

67 LEARN HOW TO MAXIMISE YOUR MONEY-MAKING POTENTIALS

Your financial dream is your personal responsibility to pursue, grow and protect. Nobody else can do that for you. It's nobody else's business to make you reach your destiny. It's all yours. You may say, 'but nobody seems to believe in it'. That's alright. Cease seeking the approval of men. Your future is hidden in your dream. The future you've been seeking for is hidden in your dream.

You Will Only Succeed with An Obsession

When you hear the names of these people, what do you remember? Billy Graham? Salvation. Tiger woods? Golf. Barack Obama? President. Michael Jordan? Basketball. Serena Williams? Tennis. If you cannot phrase your dream in one word, you don't know it. If they are many, you have none. **The only way to kill a man with a dream is to give him a second one**, because the only reason men fail is broken focus. Confusion and unproductive life begins once you embrace a substitution to your obsession. In other words, your dream begins in your inside, not outside. It's not what your father, mother, brother, sister, spouse, nor friends want you to do, have, and/or become. Don't borrow dream from other people because it's the reason a lot of people are struggling today. Never adopt a dream that energises your family or friend. Discover the dream that excites and energises you.

It Provokes Change

Your dream determines what you are willing to change. You will hardly consider changing a relationship until your goal in life changes. Your focus doesn't change without an overwhelming dream. Your dream provokes your capability to change. It births tenacity and persistence Your dream determines what you are willing to overcome.

The Power of Your Imagination

Your mind has two functions; the memory and the imagination. The memory replays the past and the imagination pre-play the future. You have to see your future in the room of your imagination inside you first, because you have to succeed inside you before you can succeed around you. Your head has to change first before changes around you will begin. What is in your heart and head determines what is in your hand.

Everybody Will Not Agree with You

Some people might feel intimidated by it. Your dream often intimidates people who have different dreams. People naturally oppose what they do not understand and try to talk you out of it. In other words, people going nowhere wants you to go nowhere with them, so when you try to be different they get irritated. One of the most destructive people in your life is the one who feeds your doubt and make you feel like you cannot accomplish anything in life. You have to identify such dangerous relationships and disconnect from them before you can succeed. It won't be a known enemy that will stop you; it will be someone you choose to trust with your dream. If you fail with your life, I'll trace it to someone you chose to trust.

Your Financial Goal Will Require A Specific Plan

Where is your financial plan? Everyone has got a thought, but thought is not a plan. Japanese people have 100-year goals. They plan what would happen to a company 100 year from now. Some people don't even plan what's coming up next week. You must invest your time to plan. A plan is a written plan from your present to your desired future. Jesus said what a man wants to build a house does not first sit down to count the cost and see if he has enough money to finish it. You want to buy yourself a car, what is your plan? Because when you choose a goal God will give you a plan.

Your Financial Dream Will Require Patience

Patience is a weapon that forces deception to be revealed. Patience is not a delay, rather it is the weapon that forces an enemy to uncover him/herself. The ability to wait is a divine weaponry.

Your Financial Plan Will Require Passion

Pay attention to your passion, it's a sign post to where your life is going. You may not like doing paperwork, but you like teaching people. Why? The difference is passion. Passion enables you to see the shortest route to where you are going. It's passion that qualifies who belongs to your life and those who do not belong to it. Those who protect your passion are those assigned to you. Those who weaken and divide your passion do not belong to your future. Identify those who sneer and make light of your passion to achieve your purpose.

Any Financial Dream Will Require A Mentor to Achieve It

Mentorship is necessary. The achieving of your dream would require special mentorship. The mentors in your life or the absence of them are critical to your success or failure. There are five ways to predict someone's future; the fourth is to find your mentor. Your mentor is not someone who gives you advice; your mentor is the one whose advice you follow. You can't change your life until you determine the counsel you are willing to embrace. Your mentor is not your best friend, he loves you the way you are, but your mentor loves you too much to leave you the way you are. Ones best friend is comfortable with his past; but your mentor is only comfortable with your future. Best friends can accommodate your weakness; a mentor will drive your weakness away from you. It matters at whose feet you sit. The suggestion of your mentor is a command to the protégé.

Your Financial Dream Births Hope Within You

When everything seems wrong, hope is the invisible companion beside you. Your dream keeps the bitterness out of you. Hope reminds you that anything you are going through is preparing you for what and where Providence is bringing you into. There is expiring date for every challenge facing you. In other words, if you are not where you belong, you are preparing to get there. You are either in preparation or you are already at your destination.

There Are Enemies to Your Financial Dream

Any announcement of your dream will often agitate potential adversaries. However, enemies are as necessary as friends, because you are only rewarded for the enemy you conquer. All somebody is, is a nobody who decides to take on an enemy. Therefore, get excited when an adversary enters your life, because the presence of an enemy is an announcement that the benefits of your present season is over, and your new season has begun, and your adversary is your gateway into it. An enemy is not a wall, he is a gate to the next season of your life. The size of your enemy determines the size of your reward.

Your Financial Dream Repels Mediocrity

Your dream always intimidates those lacking your boldness and passion, and it creates distance. When you have a dream in front of you, and you embrace it, those who use to be comfortable with you will move away from you. If you keep talking of your future, yesterday people will find you unbearable, but get excited because those who do not belong to your future are being weeded out.

Don't Neglect Your Financial Dream

If you neglect your dream within you, it will eventually die and buried. Your mouth and mind are magnifiers of the dream. God gave you the mouth and the mind to magnify the invisible thing inside you. Let your dream be your most loyal friend. Your most cherished dream will become your only loyal companion throughout your lifetime. Relatives will not always believe in your dream, but your dream will remain loyal to you. When everybody had walked out of your life, your dream will be there with and for you.

Your Financial Dream Will Help Set Your Priorities

It is your dream that determines what you do first every morning. Your schedules as a matter of vital importance should be set by the dream inside you, not circumstances of your life, because what you do first determines what comes second.

7

THE LAWS OF MONEY

Place and self-image are vital in the money-making equation

Financial insight is as important as any subject of study. Where you are matters as much as what you are. How you see yourself is more important than how others see you.

In America they took a group of children and put them in a class by themselves, and the teacher told the children; we have taken some test and found you to have much greater intellect. You are smarter than all other students combined, so we are going teach you differently. They started teaching them in a class by themselves and intellectually they soared up, and their grades went up like geniuses. The fact was not the test because there was none, they were not extra smart, nor did they have extra intelligence. They wanted to see how children would react if they could see themselves differently, and their minds were released.

You can only produce relatively the 'you' that you can see.

Your mind is your servant, but can rule over you

You cannot have a great life unless you have a pure life, you cannot have a pure life unless you have a pure mind, and you cannot have a pure mind unless you wash your mind daily in the word of God.

Your mind is a magnet for;

- Doubt
- Fear
- Lust

- Greed
- Disease
- Bitterness
- Anxiety

They took nine football players in America and told them they have a disease in their body. Seven days later, two of them could not move. They have become completely paralysed from their waist down. Every one of them developed pain in their body. But they have only done test on the power of words. They told them at the end, nothing was wrong with them, other than the fact that they told them they have a disease, and their minds took it and magnified it, until their whole body embraced it. Change is proportional to knowledge.

Financial Understanding

Many of us operate by instruction, when someone tells us what to do, we go ahead to do it without knowing why we are doing it. So we fault and loose the benefit of understanding. Hence, it's not enough to follow an instruction, but must be done with understanding.

Financial Wisdom

The difference between seasons in your life is your wisdom; the difference between prosperity and poverty is wisdom; the difference between a happy marriage and unhappy marriage is your wisdom. The difference between the rich and the poor is wisdom.

You will never have a financial problem. You do not have a marriage problem. What you have is a wisdom problem. How? If you think you have a financial problem, you continue to change jobs. If you think you have a marriage problem, you change mates. Money is not the cure for financial problem. Your problem is lack of wisdom to handle money. Study the entry and exit of money.

When you recognise you have a wisdom problem you will begin to change your focus, to correct your life, to seek your proper place in life.

Wisdom is progressive, but not generic. It does not come to bloodline, or to nationalities. Wisdom is a decision. Wisdom is produced through humility. Humility is the recognition of what you do not have. Confidence is as a result of what you do have.

Your decisions have created your circumstances

Unless you understand this, you can spend the rest of your life blaming others including God for your circumstances. You will become retaliatory, angry and vindictive. If I believed others were responsible for my circumstances, then this belief system will force me to wait until they change so that my own circumstances would change. That's what creates bitterness. But the moment I realise and embrace I can do something about my circumstances; something in me begins to change.

Nobody can help you if you do not have a desire, a conclusion you are focused on. It's not enough to hate your past, you got have the picture of your future, because you can't leave where you are until you have a photograph of where you would rather be. It's not enough to hate your present you have to know the future you desire.

83 LEARN HOW TO MAXIMISE YOUR MONEY-MAKING POTENTIALS

www.ingramcontent.com/pod-product-compliance
Lightning Source LLC
Chambersburg PA
CBHW020454220526
45464CB00002B/981